KT-226-824

CONTENTS

SYMBOLS KEY

The following symbols are used throughout this book:

ⓐ address ❶ telephone ❶ fax ⓦ website address ⓔ email
🕒 opening times ⓝ public transport connections ❶ important

The following symbols are used on the maps:

𝒊 information office		○	city
✈ airport		○	large town
✚ hospital		○	small town
🛡 police station		=	motorway
🚌 bus station		—	main road
🚆 railway station		—	minor road
✝ cathedral		—	railway
POI (point of interest)			
❶ numbers denote featured cafés, restaurants & venues			

PRICE CATEGORIES

The ratings below indicate average price rates for a double
room per night, including breakfast:
£ under £65 ££ £65–160 £££ over £160
The typical cost for a three-course meal without drinks,
is as follows:
£ under £20 ££ £20–40 £££ over £40

▶ King's College gates

INTRODUCING
Aberdeen

Introduction

The grand buildings of Aberdeen's historic centre are made of a mica-flecked granite stone that glitters in sunlight, hence its nickname: the Silver City. Scotland's third largest city stands at the mouth of the River Dee, on the North Sea coast. Inland lie flat farmlands of the northeast, lush woodland glens, and wild moors and mountains. Uniquely in Britain, there's a huge sandy beach right next to the city centre.

Home to one of Britain's oldest universities, Aberdeen continues to be a centre of academic and technological excellence. Traditionally a base for Scotland's fishing industry and the commercial hub of the northeast, the city has experienced dramatic change since the discovery of oil resources beneath the North Sea in the mid-1970s. Almost overnight, Aberdeen became a boom town, with oil business executives flying in from all over the world, while thousands of workers flocked to the city to take up well-paid jobs onshore and offshore. The oil bonanza swelled the city's population from just under 138,000 in 1971 to around 210,400 by 2008 – an expansion unparalleled in any other British city. It is claimed that the smartest residential sector of the city is home to a higher concentration of millionaires than anywhere else in the UK outside London.

New-found prosperity endowed Aberdeen with smart new bars, clubs and restaurants, while the oil industry's needs also fostered new air routes and luxury hotels, making the city much more accessible and tourist-friendly, and also transforming it into a more cosmopolitan place. According to the 2008 census,

15.7 per cent of its population were born outside Scotland, significantly higher than the national average.

But despite these changes, Aberdeen in the 21st century is still fiercely proud of its identity, symbolised by grand historic buildings, a distinctive regional dialect and rich traditions. Furthermore, less than an hour's journey away from the city centre limits lies a collection of heritage attractions ranging from medieval castles to ancient stone circles, and areas of natural beauty including the wooded valley of Royal Deeside, the dramatic wilderness of the Cairngorms National Park, sea-girt cliffs and sweeping sandy beaches. Aberdeen is more than just a great city to visit in its own right: it's also a perfect gateway to one of Scotland's most underrated regions.

⏺ *Lavish flower beds at the Union Terrace Gardens*

When to go

Aberdeen can be visited year round, and demand from business travellers and academic visitors ensures that its hotels and other visitor services stay open all year, as do all the city's visitor attractions. The sights of the compact city centre are close together, so even in winter the visitor needn't be exposed to the elements for long. Cold, wet weather is common from November to April, and it can rain at any time of year, but overall the local microclimate is surprisingly mild, which has no doubt helped Aberdeen to win the annual Britain in Bloom competition ten times.

However, the best times to visit are undoubtedly between June and September, when long summer days compensate for occasional showers: this far north, there are only around five hours of darkness in midsummer. Summer daytime temperatures average between 10°C (50°F) and 18°C (64°F) in July and August (the warmest months of the year) and from 0°C (32°F) to 6°C (43°F) in January, the coldest month. That said, record highs of 27°C (81°F) have been recorded in July and August and of 17°C (63°F) in January and February, and a record low of –18°C (–0.4°F) has been noted in January.

Aberdeen and the surrounding region play host to a year-round calendar of festivals. In March, the **Aberdeen Jazz Festival** (ⓦ www.jazzaberdeen.com) features leading contemporary jazz artists from all over the world and has become one of Britain's top jazz events. **Rootin Aboot** (ⓦ www.lemontree.org), in April, celebrates the folk music of the northeast but also hosts blues, Indian, African, Latin American, bluegrass, dance and rock

▲ *An oasis of green and calm in a bustling city: Duthie Park Gardens*

performances. **Triptych** (ⓦ www.triptychfestival.com) is an exciting contemporary music festival held in Scotland's three largest cities, including Aberdeen. Summer events include **WORD** (ⓦ www.abdn.ac.uk/word), a major event on the Scottish literary scene; the one-day **Taste of Grampian** food festival (www.tasteofgrampian.co.uk); the **City of Aberdeen Highland Games** (ⓦ www.aberdeencity.gov.uk); and the colourful ten-day **Aberdeen International Youth Festival**. November is brightened up by another contemporary music festival, **Sound** (ⓦ www.sound-scotland.co.uk), and the annual fireworks display, and the year is wound up in traditional Scottish style with the city's **Hogmanay Street Party** on New Year's Eve. Details of more events in and around Aberdeen throughout the year can be found at ⓦ www.visitaberdeen.com

History

The history of Aberdeen as a city began with the granting of a charter by William the Lion in 1179; in 1319, Robert the Bruce gave the city the status of a Royal Burgh. For the next four centuries, the city's history was occasionally turbulent. It was sacked by Edward III of England in 1336, and suffered devastation during the Civil Wars of 1644–47, but between these violent interludes Aberdeen thrived, developing a healthy trade with Scandinavia and the Baltic.

For much of its history from the late 12th century, Aberdeen's noble patrons and defenders were the Keiths, Earls Marischal of Scotland. Their line died out when George, the 10th Earl Marischal

🔶 *St Machar's Cathedral: an ancient place of Christian worship*

ABERDEEN'S TWO UNIVERSITIES

Aberdeen has been a centre of learning for more than 500 years, since the foundation of King's College by the Bishop of Aberdeen, William Elphinstone, in 1495. George Keith, the 5th Earl Marischal of Scotland, founded Marischal College in 1593, and the two colleges merged into the University of Aberdeen in 1860. The city's other university was founded by a wealthy merchant, Robert Gordon, in 1729 as a trades college, and was reborn as Robert Gordon University in 1992.

(1693–1778), picked the losing side during the 1715 Jacobite Rising and forfeited his title. Despite siding with the Jacobite cause (the fight to restore the Stuarts to the British throne), Aberdeen survived the 1715 and the later 1745 risings unscathed, and over the next century it became a major fishing port and shipbuilding centre. Fishing boomed during the late 19th century onwards, and Aberdeen's trawler fleet became one of the largest in Britain.

Over-fishing pushed the North Sea fishery into decline in the second half of the 20th century, however, so the discovery of oil in the mid-1970s came as a lifeline to the city. Today, oil still dominates, and new discoveries beneath the Moray Firth have given the local oil industry a further boost. However, oil stocks will not last forever, and Aberdeen is making a conscious effort to diversify and strengthen its position as a centre of learning and new technologies.

Culture

Aberdeen's cultural scene embraces the written and spoken word, traditional and classical music, the visual arts, cinema and theatre, and the city's historic landmarks include some of the finest examples of medieval Scottish architecture.

Internationally renowned natives of the city and the surrounding region include musicians such as rock diva Annie Lennox, solo percussionist and composer Dame Evelyn Glennie, vocalist Sandi Thom, Colin Angus of The Shamen and Billy Bremner of Rockpile. With a youthful population and a large student body, Aberdeen also has a popular indie music scene.

The traditional music of Aberdeen and the northeast has experienced a huge renaissance over the last 30 years and is celebrated at traditional and world music festivals in and around the city. The distinctive Doric dialect of Aberdeen and the northeast has also enjoyed a recent revival as a medium for lyrics, verse and the written word and is celebrated at events such as the annual WORD Festival.

Aberdeen and its surroundings inspire a number of contemporary painters, printmakers, videomakers and photographers including Iain Carby, whose gallery displays his own striking landscapes and seascapes as well as works by other local artists.

▶ *The spectacular David Welch Winter Gardens, full of tropical plants*

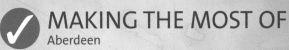 **MAKING THE MOST OF**
Aberdeen

Shopping

Aberdeen is the major shopping centre for northeast Scotland. With more than its fair share of resident millionaires, the city has shops that cater for all needs, tastes and budgets.

SHOPPING AREAS

Union Street, which runs roughly southwest to northeast through the city centre, is the city's main shopping street. For a quirkier, more individual shopping experience, head for **The Green**, one block south of Union Street. This historic and increasingly trendy part of the old city boasts a growing number of designer boutiques. More smart shops can be found in the West End area of the city, around the more upmarket western end of Union Street.

SHOPPING CENTRES

Aberdeen's flagship mall is the Union Square shopping centre (ⓦ www.unionsquareaberdeen.com) which opened in 2009. It houses more than 60 stores, plus around a dozen fast-food restaurants and cafés. As part of the ambitious Bon Accord Quarter Masterplan, which aims to completely revitalise the city's main retail area, the Bon Accord and St Nicholas shopping centres (ⓦ www.stnicholasandbonaccord.com), between School Hill and Gallowgate, have been merged into one giant new mall featuring brands such as Jo Malone, Karen Millen, Hobbs and John Lewis.

MARKETS

Aberdeen's long-established **Indoor Market** is a landmark at the corner of Union Street and Market Street, with access from both streets. It has more than 500 sq m (5,300 sq ft) of stall space, with traders mostly supplying everyday needs at bargain prices. Open-air markets include the **Aberdeen Country Fair**, which is a great place to visit if you want to stock up on local delicacies or take a look at some of the crafts of Aberdeen and the surrounding area. With 35 stalls, it is held on the first and last Saturday of every month on Belmont Street. Even more cosmopolitan is the **International Street Market**, which is held in Union Terrace three times yearly (spring, summer and autumn) over three days and attracts traders from more than a dozen European countries.

🔺 *Head to Union Street for some retail therapy*

Eating & drinking

Aberdeen has shared in the Scottish culinary revolution since the 1990s. The city now has some of the best restaurants in Scotland, serving the best of regionally sourced lamb, beef, game and seafood. There's a wide spectrum of international restaurants too, including Chinese, Indian, Japanese, Italian and French eating places.

Aberdeen still has its share of old-fashioned bars, but it also has plenty of up-to-date alternatives, including smart cocktail bars, bistros and café-bars. **Belmont Street**, in the city centre, is a main focus of the eating and drinking scene.

⬤ *Belmont Street is where you'll find something for every appetite*

Despite the advent of kebabs and burger joints, Aberdeen's traditional fish and chip shops continue to flourish. On a sunny summer evening, a fish supper eaten while looking out to sea is a simply perfect eating experience.

It is not usual to leave a tip in self-service bars, pubs and cafés, although tipping is increasingly expected in smarter bar-restaurants and a tip of 10 per cent is appropriate (where the service and the food merits it) in more formal eating places and hotel restaurants.

Smoking has been banned in all restaurants, cafés, bars and pubs in Scotland since 2006, so many establishments now provide an outdoor seating area (sometimes even warmed by gas heaters) for real tobacco addicts. Some bars open as early as 10.00; others stay open until 03.00 or even 04.00. More normal opening hours are 11.00–23.00 Monday–Saturday and 12.00–22.30 on Sunday for most pubs and bars, and from 12.00–15.00 and 19.00–24.00 for most restaurants. Shorter opening hours apply on Sundays, when some upmarket restaurants may be closed or open only for lunch.

PICNIC PLACES

Weather permitting, Aberdeen is well supplied with parks and other places for a picnic. Between Old Aberdeen and the River Don (just north of St Machar's Cathedral), Seaton Park is a congenial green space, and the sandy beach, only a few minutes' walk from the city centre, is perfect for an alfresco snack on a sunny day.

Entertainment

Aberdeen is a lively city after dark with entertainment that spans the spectrum from the latest indie sounds to dance, drama, classical music, opera and folk music. For film lovers, there are several large, modern cinemas, including a huge, ten-screen **Cineworld** in the Union Square retail complex. Purpose-built venues around the city play host to performances by visiting theatre companies, jazz and rock bands, and the touring Scottish Opera and Scottish Ballet ensembles, as well as international artists.

The city's landmark venues include the **Aberdeen Music Hall**, on Union Street, which was designed by Aberdeen's most famous architect, Archibald Simpson, and opened in 1822. Likewise, **His Majesty's Theatre**, which opened in 1906, is a

---

TICKETS & INFORMATION

For day-to-day information on what's on where in Aberdeen, see the listings and classified advertisements in the daily *Press and Journal* and *Evening Express* newspapers. Tickets for performances at most major venues can be bought from the Aberdeen Box Office online at Ⓦ www.boxofficeaberdeen.com Ⓣ tel: 01224 641122. For news of the indie and club scene, pick up a copy of *The Skinny* ('the underground guide to what's on across Scotland') in trendier, student-orientated bars and pubs or visit Ⓦ www.theskinny.co.uk

significant landmark of the city's architectural heritage. To mark its centenary it underwent an £8m refurbishment, which reaffirmed its status as the city's iconic performance space.

But Aberdeen isn't all about grand theatres and giant cinema complexes. On a cosier, more intimate level, there are live music bars that welcome jazz players and acoustic musicians, pubs which feature lively ceilidh nights (Scottish music and dancing) and the traditional music of northeast Scotland, and arts centres dedicated to fostering a diverse range of experimental theatre, live music and comedy.

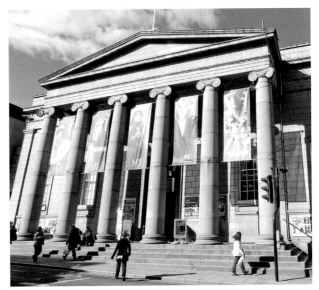

⬤ *Aberdeen's impressive Music Hall*

Sport & relaxation

SPECTATOR SPORTS

Cricket

Cricket is popular in Aberdeen and the northeast, with 25 local clubs, the most important of which is Aberdeenshire CC.

Aberdeenshire Cricket Club ⓐ Morningside Road, Mannofield ⓘ 01224 317888 ⓦ www.aberdeenshirecc.org.uk ⓒ contact club for fixtures ⓝ Bus: 16, 16A, 19 ⓘ Admission charge

Football

Football is Aberdeen's most popular spectator sport.

Aberdeen FC, Pittodrie Stadium ⓐ Pittodrie St ⓣ 01224 631903 ⓦ www.afc.co.uk ⓔ feedback@afc.co.uk ⓒ contact club for fixtures ⓝ Bus: 1, 1A, 2, 2A, 15 ⓘ Admission charge

PARTICIPATION SPORTS

Golf

In northeast Scotland, golf is high on the sporting agenda. There are half a dozen golf courses in the Aberdeen area. The **Royal Aberdeen Golf Club** and **King's Links Golf Centre** are the two courses closest to the city centre. See pages 71–2 for details.

Skating

Linx Ice Arena Skating and in-line skating are available at this state-of-the-art ice centre. ⓐ Beach Promenade ⓣ 01224 655406 ⓦ www.aberdeencity.gov.uk ⓒ 10.00–12.00, 12.30–15.00 & 19.30–21.30 Mon, Tues & Fri, 12.00–14.00 Wed & Thur, 15.00–17.00 Sat & Sun. Call to check. ⓝ Bus: 13A ⓘ Admission charge

◔ *Practise your swing at the Royal Aberdeen Golf Course*

Spas

The Marcliffe Hotel's luxury spa ⓐ North Deeside Rd
ⓣ 01224 861000 ⓦ www.marcliffe.com ⓔ info@marcliffe.com
ⓛ 10.00–18.00 Mon–Wed, 10.00–20.00 Thur & Fri, 09.30–17.00
Sat, 10.00–17.00 Sun ❶ Admission charge

Swimming

Aberdeen has several public swimming pools (see
ⓦ www.aberdeencity.gov.uk). For visitors, the **Beach Leisure
Centre** is the most accessible and has four flumes, rapids and a
wave machine. ⓐ Beach Promenade ⓣ 01224 655401
ⓦ www.aberdeencity.gov.uk ⓛ public sessions 16.00–20.00 Mon
& Wed, 12.00–20.00 Tue & Thur, 16.00–17.00 Fri, 10.00–17.00 Sat,
13.00–17.00 Sun ⓝ Bus: 13A ❶ Admission charge

Accommodation

As Europe's energy industry capital, Aberdeen attracts large numbers of business travellers, so main hotel groups such as Holiday Inn, Marriott, Hilton, Thistle and Jury's Inn have a presence in the city to cater for them. The city also has a number of independent and luxurious boutique hotels. A recent trend has been the appearance of a number of self-catering 'aparthotels', which offer very good value for families or groups of friends, with fully equipped kitchens, living rooms and one or more bedrooms. At the budget end, there are plenty of well-appointed small guesthouses and bed and breakfast establishments, and one high-quality youth hostel. Almost all hotels and guesthouses stay open all year round. If you're looking for upmarket accommodation, reserve your room well ahead, since Aberdeen hosts numerous business meetings, exhibitions and conferences that create a high demand for rooms in business-orientated hotels.

Aberdeen Youth Hostel £ Comfortable youth hostel in a dignified old house, less than 3 km (2 miles) from the station and city centre. Bunks in small dorms, family rooms and private twin rooms are available, as is breakfast. ⓐ 8 Queen's Road ⓣ 01224 646988 ⓦ www.syha.org.uk ⓔ reservations@syha.org.uk ⓝ Bus: 14, X15, X17

Express by Holiday Inn £ Modern, functional facilities more than compensate for this chain hotel's slightly bland character, and it certainly offers superb value for money, with plenty of places to eat, drink and be entertained right on its doorstep. ⓐ Chapel Street ⓣ 01224 623500 ⓦ www.hieaberdeen.co.uk ⓔ info@hieaberdeen.co.uk ⓝ Bus: 14, X15, X17

Atholl Hotel ££ This cosy small hotel prides itself on offering a traditionally friendly Aberdonian welcome. Rooms are modern but with character, and the restaurant, which concentrates on traditional Scots cooking and locally sourced ingredients, attracts plenty of locals as well as visitors – always a good sign. ⓐ 54 King's Gate ⓣ 01224 323505 ⓦ www.atholl-aberdeen.com ⓔ info@atholl-aberdeen.com ⓝ Bus: 13, 13A

Brentwood Hotel ££ Townhouse hotel with 64 rooms in the city centre. Bedrooms are comfortable enough, though the overall look is a bit bland. Very well priced for what you get, with bargain rates available at weekends. ⓐ 101 Crown Street ⓣ 01224 595440 ⓦ www.brentwood-hotel.co.uk ⓔ reservations@brentwood-hotel.co.uk ⓝ Bus: 13, 13A

Chapel Apartments ££ A collection of one-bedroom apartments, each with a roomy lounge area and open-plan kitchen. With a comfy sofa to curl up on after a hard day's sightseeing, in front of a big-screen TV, they provide a real home away from home in the heart of the city. ⓐ 49 Chapel Street ⓣ 07824 666231 ⓦ www.chapelapartments.com ⓔ melissarosso5@aol.com ⓝ Bus: 14, X15, X17

City Wharf Apartments ££ Comfortable, serviced apartments with one to four bedrooms at two city-centre locations (one by the harbour, the other just south of Union Street). Facilities include fully fitted kitchen, daily maid service and free access to a nearby health club and swimming pool. ⓐ 19–21 Regent Quay and 31–32 Springbank Terrace ⓣ 08450 942942 ⓦ www.citywharfapartments.co.uk ⓔ reservations@citywharfapartments.co.uk ⓝ Bus: 3, 5, 12, 59; railway and bus stations within easy walking distance.

The Globe Inn ££ The Globe Inn is a one-stop-shop for good pub food and drink (with barbecues in its beer garden in summer), entertainment (live bands every Friday and Saturday night, traditional folk sessions on Tuesday) and comfortable, well-appointed en-suite rooms. ⓐ 15 Silver Street ⓣ 01224 624658 ⓦ www.the-globe-inn.co.uk ⓔ info@the-globe-inn.co.uk ⓝ Bus: 3,10,25

Micasa ApartHotel ££ Don't be fooled by the Georgian exterior. Behind the façade of this gracious building are 34 hip and funky apartments, each with a modern kitchen, spacious living room and comfortable bedrooms. Continental breakfast is included in the rate, and there is a 24-hour reception desk. ⓐ 9 Market Street ⓣ 01224 565950 ⓦ www.micasaaparthotel.co.uk ⓔ info@micasaaparthotel.co.uk ⓝ Bus: 3, 5, 12, 59; railway and bus stations within easy walking distance.

Skene House ££ Skene House offers its 'hotelsuites' at three city addresses. Skene House Holburn is the most centrally located, but the other two are also conveniently close to sights and attractions. The suites have 1–3 bedrooms, sitting room and kitchen. ⓐ 6 Union Grove; 2 Whitehall Place; 96 Rosemount Viaduct ⓣ 01224 646600 ⓦ www.skene-house.co.uk ⓔ whitehall@skene-house.co.uk ⓝ Bus: 13, 13A

The Carmelite £££ If the girls from *Sex and the City* ever came to Aberdeen, this is where they'd want to stay – in one of the six impressive suites with trimmings such as monsoon shower and plasma TV. Designer rooms are similarly stylish, while standard rooms share the overall trendy ambience, as do public areas, including the Carmelite Bar and Grill, which has a contemporary menu that emphasises fresh seafood, and live music at weekends. ⓐ Stirling Street ⓣ 01224 589101 ⓦ www.carmelitehotels.com ⓔ contact@carmelitehotels.com ⓝ Bus: 3, 5, 12, 59; railway and bus stations within 90 m (100 yds)

Malmaison £££ Opened in 2008, Malmaison brought all the components of this boutique hotel chain to Aberdeen: stylish bar, excellent restaurant, and sybaritically comfortable bedrooms with quirky trimmings. Highly recommended. ⓐ 49–53 Queens Road ⓣ 01224 327370 ⓦ www.malmaison.com ⓔ info.aberdeen@malmaison.com ⓝ Bus: 14, X15, X17

Norwood Hall Hotel £££ The perfect hideaway for those looking for peace, quiet and a bit of grandeur, within easy reach of the city centre. With its pillared portico opening into an equally grand interior, award-winning restaurant, and 3 hectares (7 acres) of wooded grounds, it blends character with comfort. ⓐ Garthdee Road ⓣ 01224 868951 ⓦ www.norwood-hall.co.uk ⓔ reservations@norwood-hall.co.uk ⓝ Bus: 203, 202, 201

THE BEST OF ABERDEEN

Aberdeen is a small city with a compact historic centre, so it's pleasingly easy to visit all its main sights on foot.

TOP 10 ATTRACTIONS

- **King's College** Founded in the 15th century, the college's campus is surrounded by a collection of dignified historic buildings built in the city's hallmark granite stone (see page 63).

- **St Machar's Cathedral** According to local legend, this cathedral was built on the site of one of Britain's oldest Christian places of worship (see page 64).

- **Aberdeen Maritime Museum** Rediscover Aberdeen's history as one of Europe's great fishing, trading and shipbuilding ports (see page 73).

- **Kirk of St Nicholas** The history of this medieval place of worship is intimately tied up with the city's own past (see page 45).

- **Satrosphere Science Centre** Discover Aberdeen's role as a cutting-edge centre of technology and science at this exciting visitor attraction (see pages 73–4).

- **Provost Skene's House** Walk back into history within this 16th-century building, with its Painted Gallery, Costume Gallery and period rooms furnished with antiques (see page 47).

- **Aberdeen Jazz Festival** Jazz musicians and singers from all over the world flock to Aberdeen for this annual musical event (see page 8).

- **City of Aberdeen Highland Games** Pipe music, Highland dancers and kilted muscle-men competing at sports such as tossing the caber, throwing the hammer and tug o' war (see page 9).

- **Aberdeen Beach** A great place for a summer picnic or a bracing winter walk (see page 69).

- **Dunnottar Castle** Perched on a crag above the sea, Dunnottar is, in its forbidding way, one of Scotland's most spectacular castles (see page 70).

⬇ *Enjoy the music, dancing and sports at the Highland Games*

Suggested itineraries

HALF DAY: ABERDEEN IN A HURRY

Old Aberdeen's treasury of medieval architecture is just a few steps from the city centre. High points of the medieval university quarter are **King's College** itself, **Elphinstone Hall** and the **Old Town House**, while **St Machar's Cathedral**, the city's other medieval icon, lies just to the north of the campus.

1 DAY: TIME TO SEE A LITTLE MORE

Take time to savour the medieval glories of Old Aberdeen, then head back into the city centre to visit the period salons of

● *William Wallace: Scottish patriot and national hero*

16th-century **Provost Skene's House**, the acclaimed **Maritime Museum** and the massive granite pile that is **Marischal College**, the world's second-largest granite building.

2–3 DAYS: DISCOVERING ABERDEEN'S OUTSKIRTS

Head past the modern harbour to **Footdee** (pronounced 'Fittie'), where rows of 19th-century fishing-folks' cottages are a charming contrast to the city centre's grander historic architecture. Take a bus south to **Dunnottar Castle**, a grim stronghold overlooking the North Sea or enjoy an afternoon of old-fashioned fun on the traditional rides at Codona's Amusement Park. If you're a golfer, you can fit in a round at one or other of the city's fine courses. For non-golfers, the sharp new boutiques around The Green may beckon.

LONGER: ENJOYING ABERDEEN AND ROYAL DEESIDE TO THE FULL

Aberdeen is more than just a great place for a city break. It's the gateway to a part of Scotland that is often overlooked, but which has much to offer. You can sign up for a one-day escorted tour of the high points of 'Royal Deeside', taking in **Ballater** and **Braemar**, the Royal Family's impressive holiday home at **Balmoral** or head to the natural beauty of the Cairngorms. Still better, rent a car for a day or two to travel at your own pace and visit the many whisky distilleries along the Speyside Whisky Trail. Some, such as Glenfiddich, produce malts that are well known the world over, while others, such as Glen Moray and Dallas Dhu, are smaller scale but still offer wonderful examples of the Scots' 'national' tipple.

Something for nothing

Something for nothing? In Aberdeen? You must be joking. The English laugh about the notoriously parsimonious Scots, but for Scots the tight-fistedness of the average Aberdonian is the stuff of legend. Aberdonians, it must be said, generally just treat this kind of mockery with weary tolerance. In reality, however, Aberdeen has a more than adequate assortment of things to do and see free of charge. Aberdeen's huge North Sea beach, of course, costs nothing at all, and you can picnic here, and even swim on a summer's day, or take a brisk and bracing walk at any time of year, as long as you're dressed for the weather.

Many of the city's publicly funded museums and art galleries also charge nothing for admission, including Provost Skene's House, the Aberdeen Art Gallery and the Aberdeen Maritime Museum (see pages 47, 49, 51 and 73).

Aberdeen has a number of beautiful public parks and gardens that are at their most beautiful in early summer when the flowers come into bloom, and in autumn as the leaves turn golden, but they can also be very attractive on a frosty winter day. The city's two big green spaces are Duthie Park on the north bank of the River Dee (see page 45) and Seaton Park on the south bank of the River Don (see pages 64–6).

When it rains

Only the luckiest visitor escapes the occasional spell of rain in Aberdeen, but fortunately the city has a wide range of places to while away a rainy day or a cold, dark winter afternoon. Obviously all the museums offer shelter from the elements, as do the church and college interiors. Next to the station, the glossy new Union Square mall (ⓦ www.unionsquareaberdeen.com) is Scotland's biggest indoor shopping centre, with more than 60 shops – including major high-street fashion and accessory brands and outlets serving more practical needs too – as well as a choice of around a dozen eating places, a 10-screen cinema and a Pure day spa.

For the more energetic, the Beach Leisure Centre (see page 21) has an indoor lagoon-style pool with four flume rides and artificial waves, a fully equipped fitness studio and saunas. For golfers driven off the links by poor weather, King's Links (see page 71) has a floodlit driving range with 56 covered and heated bays.

South of the city, on the north bank of the River Dee, the 19th-century Duthie Park offers a semi-tropical refuge from Scottish weather within the vast, glass-covered David Welch Winter Gardens, which is filled with cacti and other exotic plants.

On arrival

ARRIVING BY AIR, RAIL, ROAD, SEA

By air

Aberdeen International Airport is at Dyce, 11 km (7 miles) northwest of the city centre, with flights from London and several other British regional cities as well as international connections to numerous European capitals and resorts (see page 90). There is no rail link to the airport, and Aberdeen is notorious for its peak-hour traffic jams, so if you have an early evening flight to catch, allow plenty of time to get to the terminal; the journey, though short, can take as much as 30 minutes.

Airport buses and taxis leave from immediately outside the arrivals hall. A taxi to the centre costs almost five times as much as taking the airport bus but, for groups or families, taking a taxi is a good option. Several international car rental companies have desks at the airport (see page 40).

By rail

Aberdeen's only railway station (see page 90) is right in the centre of the city, within easy walking distance of Union Street and the harbour and ferry terminal (see By sea, opposite). Regional rail services link the city with Inverness and with other Scottish cities, including Dundee, Edinburgh and Glasgow. Long-distance trains (at least three times a day) connect Aberdeen with London and major English cities en route, and there is also a nightly sleeper service to London. There is a 24-hour taxi rank at the station.

By bus

Several regional and long-distance bus companies, including Citylink, National Express and Megabus, connect Aberdeen with other Scottish cities, including Inverness, Dundee, Stirling, Edinburgh and Glasgow. The city coach terminus (recently refurbished) is opposite the railway station. Travelling by coach is the cheapest way of getting to Aberdeen, but with a journey time of around 12 hours from London, it can be a false economy – the cheapest air fares may cost only £30–40 so flying can make more sense than going by coach.

By car

If you plan to drive to Aberdeen, the fastest route from central Scotland and the rest of the UK is the A90, via Forfar and Dundee, which is a dual carriageway for most of its length. Aberdeen is around 190 km (120 miles) – about 2½ hours' drive – north of Edinburgh, Scotland's capital. If you're making Aberdeen part of a driving tour of northern Scotland, the A96 will take you north and west, via Elgin, to Inverness, the gateway to the Highlands.

By sea

Ferry services connect Aberdeen with Stornoway in Orkney and Lerwick in Shetland. They depart from the harbour Ferry Terminal, a two-minute walk from the station and bus station. Some cruise ships also call at Aberdeen, on itineraries that may include the Orkney and Shetland Islands, the Faroe Islands, and Norwegian ports such as Bergen and Stavanger.

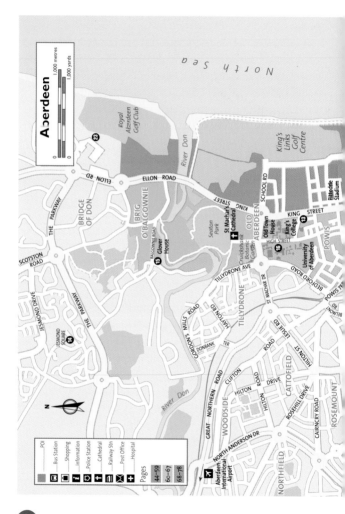

Aberdeen Bay

FOOTDEE

EAST KIRKHILL

Codona's Amusement Park

ESPLANADE

Satrosphere Science Centre

Cathedral Church of St Andrew

Aberdeen Castle

CASTLEGATE

Victoria Dock

Albert Basin

TORRY

CRAIGINCH

KING STREET

Family History Society

Marischal College

Maritime Museum

Provost Skene House

Victoria Bridge

WELLINGTON ROAD

Dunnottar Castle →

RIVERSIDE

HUTCHEON ST

GEORGE ST

Bon Accord & St Nicholas Centres

Art Gallery

MARKET ST

Union Square Shopping Centre

DRIVE

River Dee

LEWIS PLACE

ROSEMOUNT PL

James Dun's House

Johnston Gardens

Aberdeen Station

COLLEGE ST

Foyer Gallery

FERRYHILL

Duthie Park

WILLOWBANK ROAD

Gallery Heinzel

ESSLEMONT AVENUE

SKENE STREET

UNION

Bon Accord Park

HOLBURN ST

ALFORD PL

GREAT

SOUTHERN RD

RIVERSIDE DRIVE

WHITEHALL PL

CARDEN PLACE

ALBYN PLACE

HOLBURN STREET

Westburn Park

WESTBURN RD

Victoria Park

BEECHGROVE TER

ARGYLL PL

ASHLEY

GREAT WESTERN ROAD

SOUTH ANDERSON DRIVE

Aberdeen Royal Infirmary

ASHGROVE ROW

FORESTHILL RD

WESTBURN ROAD

MID STOCKET ROAD

QUEEN'S CROSS

MANNOFIELD

GARTHDEE

Robert Gordon University →

NORTH ANDERSON DRIVE

ANDERSON DR

Rubislaw Quarry

GREAT WESTERN ROAD

FINDING YOUR FEET

Arriving by rail or bus, you'll find yourself just a few steps from the heart of the city. The **Aberdeen Visitor Information Centre** on Union Street, just a minute's walk from the city's train and bus stations, should be your first stop for the latest information on getting around the city. Aberdeen is a walker-friendly city and there are ambitious plans to create wider pedestrian-only areas within the city centre.

Most of the time, and in most places, Aberdeen is a fairly safe city for the visitor, and crimes involving tourists are as rare as anywhere else in Britain. However, it does have a worryingly high violent crime rate, owing mainly to alcohol-related fighting between local youths in the city centre's most popular nightlife areas, especially late at night during the weekends.

ORIENTATION

Aberdeen's city centre lies just north of the River Dee, which flows into Aberdeen Harbour. To the east of the centre lies the North Sea and the long sandy sweep of Aberdeen Beach, which ends at the mouth of the River Don.

Union Street, the city centre's main shopping street and commercial thoroughfare, runs roughly northeast–southwest, with the Town Hall and the 19th-century St Andrew's Cathedral at the northeast end. **Market Street** runs between Union Street and the harbour, and the railway station and bus station are off **Guild Street**, one block south of Union Street.

Between the city centre and the south bank of the Don is **Old Aberdeen**, the city's medieval heart, which is still dominated by the historic campus of Aberdeen University. The city's other

◆ Aberdeen's railway station

venerable academic institution, Robert Gordon University has several departments, but in the city centre. Its main campus is on the north bank of the River Dee, in the suburb of Garthdee. Residential suburbs surround the city centre, while the modern Aberdeen Science and Technology Park is located across the winding River Don, north of Old Aberdeen.

GETTING AROUND
Buses

Three bus companies, Bain's Coaches (ⓦ www.bainscoaches. co.uk), First (ⓦ firstgroup.com), and Stagecoach Bluebird (ⓦ stagecoachbus.com) operate a comprehensive network throughout the city and the surrounding area, including a night-bus schedule which operates after midnight. In the city centre, bus stops for most routes are clustered on the easternmost block of Union Street, just north of the railway station and the

◆ *A fabulous view of Aberdeen harbour at dusk*

coach station. Buy tickets from the driver on boarding. You must pay the exact fare. Alternatively, buy a Travelcard for use on First Buses, sold at the coach and railway stations, city centre Visitor Information Centre and at most local shops and newsagents.

Taxis

Taxis (some are London-style black cabs, others are saloon cars identifiable by their rooftop, light-up taxi signs) are plentiful on city-centre streets virtually 24 hours a day. They can be flagged down on the street if their amber 'For Hire' sign is lit up. You'll also find them at the main city-centre rank outside the railway station and opposite the bus station. Note that queues for taxis are longer after 23.00. All fares are metered and the cost is clearly displayed on a digital meter. Standard taxis may carry a maximum of four passengers; however, most taxi firms also operate 'people-carrier' minibus-style taxis for up to seven

people. Wheelchair-accessible taxis are also widely available, though you may need to telephone in advance to ensure your car has wheelchair access. For those who prefer to travel in style, chauffeur-driven cars and rock-star-style stretch limos can also be booked from some taxi firms.

Car hire

Renting a car is not worthwhile if you're only planning to stay in the city, but it's an excellent option if you want to make the most of your visit by seeing some more of northeast Scotland at your own pace. Roads are good and well signposted, with key visitor attractions, tourist routes and historic sights awarded their own conspicuous white-on-brown signs.

International car rental agencies with desks at Aberdeen Airport include:

Avis (www.avis.co.uk); **Hertz** (Ⓦ www.hertz.co.uk); **Europcar** (Ⓦ www.europcar.co.uk); **Alamo** (Ⓦ www.alamo.co.uk) and **Enterprise** (Ⓦ www.enterprise.co.uk).

Local car rental companies include:

Aberdeen 4x4 Self Drive ⓐ Chalmers Base, Blackburn, Aberdeen ① 01224 790858 Ⓦ www.aberdeen4x4.co.uk

Arnold Clark Car and Van Rental ⓐ Canal Road, Mounthooly, Aberdeen ① 01224 622714 Ⓦ www.arnoldclarkrental.com

Turner Hire Drive ⓐ 59 Holland Street, Aberdeen ① 01224 630730 Ⓦ www.turner-hiredrive.co.uk

U-Drive Aberdeen ⓐ 113 Constitution Street, Aberdeen ① 01224 636400 Ⓦ www.udriveaberdeen.co.uk

◗ *The Kirk of St Nicholas is one of Aberdeen's oldest places of worship*

THE CITY OF
Aberdeen

Introduction to city areas

All three areas of Aberdeen covered in the following chapters are conveniently close to each other, making Aberdeen one of Britain's easiest places to explore on foot or by public transport. It's very easy to combine some serious shopping with a walk on the beach and a dose of medieval architecture all in one morning.

Immediately north and west of the harbour is the city's main shopping area and business district, and many of the most important sights, museums and visitor attractions can be found here as well as most of the nightlife, restaurants and bars. The imposing buildings in this part of town were built in the prosperous 19th century, though there are a few medieval survivals too.

North of the modern city centre and the city ring road is the city's oldest quarter, Old Aberdeen, just south of the River Don and dominated by the granite façades of King's College and the other medieval campus buildings of one of the world's oldest universities, and by the twin spires of St Machar's Cathedral, built in the 16th century and still in use today. Naturally, the university quarter is also home to a plethora of student-orientated pubs, café-bars, shops and Internet cafés.

Aberdeen's seafront esplanade runs all the way from the quaint fishermen's cottages of Footdee, where the harbour opens into the sea, to the mouth of the River Don some 3 km (2 miles) north of the harbour. Modern wetsuits, keeping off the North Sea chill, have helped to make it into a popular spot for windsurfers and kite-surfers, and just off the esplanade are two of the city's premier sporting venues – Pittodrie Stadium, home of Aberdeen Football Club and Kings Link's Golf Course.

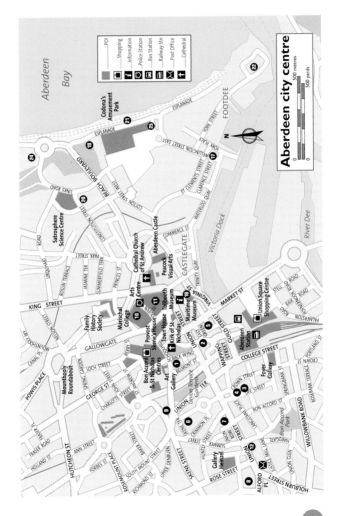

The city centre

SIGHTS & ATTRACTIONS

Castlegate

The Mercat (Market) Cross in the centre of this medieval market square identifies the Castlegate as the heart of 17th-century Aberdeen. It dates from 1686, but the miniature castle known as the Citadel on the south side of the Castlegate is a much later addition, built in 1896. ❸ Northeast end of Union Street

⬧ *Castlegate with the Citadel in the background*

Duthie Park

Duthie Park is a large park on the north bank of the Dee, complete with bandstand and cricket pitches. The David Welch Winter Gardens are also located here – a tropical greenhouse containing a variety of hothouse plants including palms and cacti. ⓐ Polmuir Road ⓣ 01224 585310 ⓛ park 08.00–dusk, gardens 09.30–18.30 daily (Apr–Sept); 09.30–15.30 daily (Oct–Mar) ⓦ Bus: 17, 21

Kirk of St Nicholas

This is one of Aberdeen's oldest places of worship, originally built in the 12th century. A later spire, built in the late 19th century, links the West Kirk with the East Kirk (which is currently closed for archaeological excavations that began in 2006). Surrounding the twin churches, the kirkyard is full of weathered tombstones, some of them bearing the spooky *memento mori* of skull and crossbones which date from early medieval times. ⓐ Union Street ⓣ 01224 643494 ⓦ www.kirk-of-st-nicholas.org.uk ⓔ office_enquiries@kirk-of-st-nicholas.org.uk ⓛ 10.00–13.00 ⓦ Bus: 6, 11, 14, 15, 23

Marischal College

One of Aberdeen's most dramatic buildings, Marischal College is scheduled to reopen as the new headquarters of Aberdeen City Council, although a date for this is yet to be set. Its elaborate granite façade, adorned with leopard-headed stone gargoyles, has been brought back to near-pristine condition after several years of cleaning to remove decades of soot and grime. The college was founded by the 4th Earl Marischal in

1593, on the site of a Franciscan friary (the Franciscans had been ejected during Scotland's Protestant Reformation). The noted Scottish architect William Adam designed a new building in the mid-18th century, but neither this nor the original friary buildings survived 70 years of rebuilding between 1836 and 1906. The reconstruction was completed to a design by Alexander Marshall Mackenzie to create the world's second-largest granite building (the largest is the Escorial, in Madrid). Mackenzie was responsible for raising the main tower to its current height of 70 m (227 ft 6 in), the elaborate façade on

⬤ *Provost Skene's House was built in the 16th century*

Broad Street and the grand Mitchell Hall. Despite this wealth of history and heritage, the building was disused for several years and was allowed to fall into disrepair. ⓐ Broad Street ⓣ 01224 274301 ⓦ www.abdn.ac.uk/marischal_museum ⓛ Contact Aberdeen University or Aberdeen City Council (aberdeencity.gov.uk) for latest information on access to Marischal College building

Provost Skene's House

Dating from 1545, this sturdy medieval townhouse was bought in 1622 by one of the city's wealthiest men, Matthew Lumsden, who commissioned the outstanding painted ceiling and had his coat of arms carved above a window in the west wing. In the late 17th century it was the home of Aberdeen's Lord Provost (equivalent to an English Mayor) George Skene. In 1746 the Duke of Cumberland billeted some of his redcoats here on the way to the Battle of Culloden. Saved from demolition in the 1930s, the building has been extensively restored, and is now Aberdeen's most involving visitor attraction, with salons and galleries that evoke the atmosphere of grand homes of the city in the 17th, 18th and 19th centuries. ⓐ Guestrow ⓣ 01224 641086 ⓕ 01224 632133 ⓦ www.aberdeencity.gov.uk ⓔ info@aagm.co.uk ⓛ 10.00–17.00 Mon–Sat, 13.00–16.00 Sun ⓝ Bus: 6, 11, 14, 15, 23

Town House

Built between 1867 and 1873 as the seat of the city's administration, the Town House is an attractive neoclassical building whose appeal is only slightly marred by a modern extension which was added in 1975–77. Within, the Town and County Hall is a grand, mock-medieval salon with a painted Flemish-style ceiling. The St Nicholas Room, too, has a stylish armorial ceiling, while the Bon Accord Room is an impressive dining hall that is used for formal dinners and other occasions hosted by Aberdeen's Lord Provost.

🅰 Union Street ☎ 01224 522637 🅦 aberdeencity.gov.uk
🅞 bgraham@aberdeencity.gov.uk 🕔 Tours 10.00–11.30 Mon–Thur, closed Fri–Sun 🅝 Bus: 6, 11, 14, 15, 23 ❶ Guided tours free by arrangement; apply in writing at least eight weeks in advance

Union Street

Union Street is the main artery of Aberdeen city centre, with several of the city's major attractions clustered at its eastern end, close to the harbour. It's more a bridge than a street, rising for much of its length on massive stone arches that span the valley of the Den Burn, a tributary stream of the River Dee. This ambitious urban project dates from 1806 and allowed the city to expand westward from its original core around the harbour.

Union Terrace Gardens

Stretching north from the arches of Union Street, this much-loved area of city-centre green space has been the subject of hot debate. In 2009 a major development company announced ambitious plans to convert the 19th-century gardens into a gleaming new shopping and residential complex, but many Aberdonians (including native-born rock diva Annie Lennox) are opposed to the project. 🅰 East side of Union Terrace, off Union Street 🕔 open 24 hrs 🅝 Bus: 6, 11, 14, 15, 23

CULTURE

Aberdeen Art Gallery

Aberdeen's art gallery is home to an outstanding portfolio of collections ranging from fine and applied art to local history, finds from prehistoric and medieval archaeological sites throughout northeast Scotland, and medieval and ancient coins which reveal the city's historic links with the broader European world. The Fine Art section, with its array of 19th- and 20th-century Scottish and English paintings, is the most immediately impressive collection, and the museum also features a growing number of works by 21st-century artists. Other highlights include an impressive holding of watercolours and etchings by Aberdeenshire-born James McBey (1883–1959), best known for his depictions of Egypt,

◆ *Union Terrace Gardens in full bloom*

● *Soak up some culture at the Aberdeen Arts Centre*

Palestine and North Africa and his iconic portrait of T E Lawrence ('Lawrence of Arabia') **ⓐ** Schoolhill **ⓣ** 01224 523700 **ⓕ** 01224 632133 **ⓦ** www.aagm.co.uk **ⓔ** info@aagm.co.uk **ⓛ** 10.00–17.00 Mon–Sat, 14.00–17.00 Sun **ⓜ** Bus: 6, 11, 14, 15, 23

Aberdeen Arts Centre

Aberdeen Arts Centre is one of the city's premier performance spaces, with an art gallery that hosts local and visiting visual artists, a café bar, and an auditorium which provides a venue for musicals, comedy, drama, and dance. **ⓐ** 33 King Street **ⓣ** 01224 635208 **ⓕ** 01224 626390 **ⓦ** www.aberdeenartscentre.org.uk **ⓔ** enquiries@ aberdeenartscentre.org.uk **ⓛ** Gallery 10.00–16.00. Open for performances; see website or call box office for dates and times of each performance **ⓜ** Bus: 6, 11, 14, 15, 23 **ⓘ** Admission charges vary

Aberdeen and North East Scotland Family History Society

This is the place to come if you are hunting for your roots in northeast Scotland, with computerised genealogical resources, records on microfilm, and expert staff who are happy to help you get started. **ⓐ** 158–164 King Street **ⓣ** 01224 646323 **ⓕ** 01224 639096 **ⓦ** www.anesfhs.org.uk **ⓔ** enquiries@ anesfhs.org.uk **ⓛ** 10.00–16.00 Mon, Wed & Thur, 10.00–16.00 and 19.00–22.00 Tues & Fri, 09.00–13.00 Sat **ⓜ** Bus: 6, 11, 14, 15, 23 **ⓘ** Free, but charges for ancestry searches

Foyer Gallery

The Foyer Restaurant in Trinity Church doubles as an art gallery which features exhibitions by different contemporary artists every couple of months, so you can combine an art viewing with a drink, lunch or dinner. Trinity Church, 82A Crown Street / 01224 582277 www.foyerrestaurant.com restaurant@aberdeenfoyer.com 11.00–23.30 Tues–Sat, closed Sun & Mon Bus: 6, 11, 14, 15, 23

Gallery Heinzel

Gallery Heinzel offers a fresh approach and a change of pace from medieval architecture and classical art, presenting instead the works of around 80 contemporary Scottish painters, printmakers, photographers and sculptors and hosting up to 10 exhibitions of new and original work each year. This is the place to go if you want to discover emerging, home-grown Scottish artistic talent. 24 Thistle Street / 01224 625629 www.galleryheinzel.com info@galleryheinzel.com 10.00–17.00 Mon–Fri, 10.00–17.30 Sat Bus: 6, 11, 14, 15, 23

Peacock Visual Arts

This is the region's key publicly funded visual arts organisation and a visit here can open your eyes to a wealth of new and established artistic talent from Aberdeen and northeast Scotland. Exhibitions change frequently and span photography, installation, video, print and paint. 21 Castle Street 01224 639539 01224 627094 www.peacockvisualarts.com info@peacockvisualarts.com 09.30–17.30 Tues–Sat, closed Sun & Mon Bus: 6, 11, 14, 15, 23

Tolbooth Museum

Aberdeen's old Tolbooth, with its 17th- and 18th-century jail cells, is one of the city's oldest buildings. Within it are displays of

◢ The Tolbooth is one of Aberdeen's oldest buildings

implements of torture, punishment and execution, including
the Maiden (a 17th-century guillotine) and a gory variety of
other instruments. The oldest parts of the Tolbooth date from
the early 17th century, but the first building on the site was
erected in the 14th century. The building was partly demolished
in the 1800s, leaving the four-storey Wardhouse tower, which
now houses the museum, and was built between 1616 and 1629.
The building is a virtual history of 400 years of Aberdeen
architecture, showing signs of alterations, demolition and
rebuilding from the 17th to the 20th centuries. Unlike more
recent buildings in the city, it is constructed mainly of
sandstone, which is easier to work than granite and so was
preferred as a building material by medieval masons.

The original Tolbooth was where the city's burghers met in
council, and where citizens and merchants paid their taxes and
tolls, hence the name. Exhibits are on show in six rooms over the
two upper floors, including the Gaoler's Room with its peep-hole
on to Union Street, the cramped Criminal Cell, the spacious Civic
Room and displays dedicated to crime and punishment, great
escapes, and the Jacobite Cell, where rebel supporters of 'Bonnie
Prince Charlie' (Charles Edward Stuart) were confined in the
aftermath of the 1745 Rising. ⓐ Castle Street ⓣ 01224 523653
ⓦ www.aagm.co.uk ⓔ info@aagm.co.uk ⓛ 10.00–16.00 Tues &
Sat, 12.30–15.30 Sun, closed Mon (July–Sept) ⓝ Bus: 6, 11, 14, 15, 23

RETAIL THERAPY

Main shopping centres in the city centre containing the best-
known high-street retailers include the new Union Square

Shopping Centre, opposite the railway station, the old-fashioned Indoor Market at the corner of Union Street and Market Street, and the Bon Accord & St Nicholas Shopping Centre between School Hill and Gallowgate. Some of the city's most attractive designer boutiques can be found in The Green, just south of Union Street, and in the West End.

Aberdeen Art Gallery Shop It's worth dropping into this attractive shop attached to the city's leading art gallery if you're looking for a postcard with real local character, prints from the gallery's collection or top-quality jewellery, pottery and glassware. ⓐ Schoolhill ⓣ 01224 523700 ⓕ 01224 632133 ⓦ www.aberdeencity.gov.uk ⓔ info@aagm.co.uk ⓛ 10.00–17.00 Mon–Sat, 14.00–17.00 Sun ⓝ Bus: 6, 11, 14, 15, 23

Alex Scott & Co The kilt has been revived as an item of Scottish menswear, and many younger Aberdonians (especially students) wear it at every opportunity, not just on formal occasions. No longer made just in traditional tartans, kilts can now be found in all kinds of pattern and material, from stripes and polka dots to denim and black leather. Alex Scott & Co has been a leading kiltmaker since 1925, and has branched out to also sell modern accessories and gifts. ⓐ 43 Schoolhill ⓣ 01224 643924 ⓦ www.kiltmakers.co.uk ⓛ 09.30–17.30 Mon–Wed, Fri & Sat, 09.30–19.00 Thur, closed Sun

Candle Close Gallery Inside a former Victorian soap factory, this arts and crafts boutique sells locally made jewellery (mainly made with semi-precious Scottish stones), woollen knitwear, antique and contemporary furniture and attractive kitchenware. 123 Gallowgate 01224 624940 www.candleclosegallery.co.uk 10.00–17.30 Mon–Fri, 09.00–17.00 Sat, 12.00–16.00 Sun

Tiso Aberdeen The Aberdeen branch of this Scotland-wide outdoor suppliers is the best place to go for all your leisure activity needs, from walking boots and insect repellent to top-quality sleeping bags, tents and backpacks. One whole room is dedicated to canoes and kayaks, another to tents of all kinds, and the staff are knowledgeable, friendly and helpful to experts and novices alike. 26 Netherkirkgate 01224 634934 www.tiso.com mail@tiso.co.uk 09.30–17.30 Mon & Tues, Thur–Sat, 10.00–17.30 Wed, 11.00–17.00 Sun

TAKING A BREAK

Books and Beans £ ❶ Near the Aberdeen Art Gallery, Books and Beans is a one-stop-shop, combining a second-hand bookshop with a fair-trade coffee shop selling excellent cakes, snacks and sandwiches as well as offering high-speed Internet access. 22 Belmont Street 01224 646438 01224 646483 www.booksandbeans.co.uk 10.30–22.00 daily Bus: 6, 11, 14, 15, 23

Café 52 £ ❷ Great imaginative snacks and light meals from a cosmopolitan menu that ranges from local favourites such as cullen skink to dishes from Asia and the Mediterranean, and a very strong list of delicious and imaginative vegetarian options.

ⓐ 52 The Green ⓣ 01224 590094 ⓦ www.cafe52.net ⓛ 18.00–24.00 Mon, 12.00–24.00 Tues–Thur, 12.00–01.00 Fri & Sat, 12.00–23.00 Sun; lunch served 12.00–15.00 ⓝ Bus: 6, 11, 14, 15, 23

Foyer Restaurant £–££ ❸ This restaurant-cum-art gallery is a light and airy space where you can relax over a drink and a snack or eat a full-scale lunch or dinner. The no-nonsense menu has some great salads and delectable puddings. ⓐ 82A Crown Street ⓣ 01224 582777 ⓦ www.foyerrestaurant.com ⓔ restaurant@ aberdeenfoyer.com ⓛ 11.00–23.30, lunch served 11.00–17.00 ⓝ Bus: 6, 11, 14, 15, 23

Café Bohème Restaurant ££ ❹ One of the smarter spots to eat in this part of town, with a French chef and a menu full of Gallic flavour. Ideal for a candlelit, romantic dinner à deux. Excellent seafood. ⓐ 23 Windmill Brae ⓣ 01224 210677 ⓦ www.cafebohemerestaurant.co.uk ⓔ info@ cafebohemerestaurant.co.uk ⓛ 12.00–14.00 & 18.00–24.00 Tues–Sat, closed Sun & Mon ⓝ Bus: 6, 11, 14, 15, 23

Carmelite Bar & Grill ££ ❺ Kenny Smart, head chef at this trendy, relaxed bistro in one of the city's hip new hotels, prides himself on his use of local produce such as Aberdeenshire lamb and pork, lamb from Shetland and freshly caught seafood. Food is served all day, and there's live music on Saturday evenings and Sunday afternoons. ⓐ Stirling Street ⓣ 01224 589101 ⓕ 01224 574288 ⓦ www.carmelitehotels.com ⓛ Food served 07.00–22.00 Mon–Sat, 07.00–20.00 Sun ⓝ Bus: 6, 11, 14, 15, 23

Stage Door Restaurant ££ ❶ Close to both Aberdeen Music Hall and His Majesty's Theatre, the Stage Door features two- and three-course pre-theatre set menus as well as an *à la carte* menu that concentrates on traditional Scots dishes with a continental twist. The steaks are excellent, and it's a popular venue for college graduation lunches and other celebrations ⓐ 26 North Silver Street ❶ 01224 642111 ❶ 01224 634466 ⓦ www.pbdevco.com ⓔ events@pbdevco.com ❶ Tues–Sat 17.00–02.00 Ⓝ Bus: 6, 11, 14, 15, 23

AFTER DARK

Aberdeen Music Hall ❼ Designed by the ubiquitous Archibald Simpson, architect of Balmoral Castle and many Aberdeen landmark buildings, Aberdeen Music Hall has played a key part on the city's entertainment scene since it opened in 1822. It now hosts visiting musical productions, pop and orchestral concerts and college graduation ceremonies. ⓐ Union Street ❶ 01224 641122 ⓦ www.musichallaberdeen.com ⓔ info@aberdeenperformingarts.com ❶ Open for performances Ⓝ Bus: 6, 11, 14, 15, 23 ❶ Admission charge for performances

Babylon ❽ Dramatic Gothic gloom suffuses the atmosphere of this intimate dance club located within the walls of a former medieval monastery. Babylon is one of the city's best nightspots, with an eclectic music policy that embraces everything from funky house to classic anthems. ⓐ 9 Alford Place ❶ 01224 595001 ⓦ www.pbdevco.com ⓔ events@pbdevco.com ❶ 23.00–03.00 Fri & Sat Ⓝ Bus: 6, 11, 14, 15, 23 ❶ Admission charge

His Majesty's Theatre ❾ This landmark venue opened in 1906 and was extensively refurbished to mark its centenary, with the addition of a new restaurant, café and bar. His Majesty's attracts major opera, ballet, musicals and dramatic performances as well as performances by local ensembles. ⓐ Rosemount Viaduct ⓣ 01224 641122 ⓦ www.htmaberdeen.com ⓔ info@aberdeenperformingarts.com ⓛ For performance times see website ⓝ Bus: 3, 10, 25 ⓘ Admission charge for performances

The Lemon Tree ❿ This lively arts venue hosts established bands and new talent as well as dance, theatre and comedy events. ⓐ 5 West North Street ⓣ 01224 642230 ⓦ www.boxofficeaberdeen.com ⓔ 01224 641122 ⓛ 10.00–23.00 Mon–Sat, closed Sun ⓝ Bus: 6, 11, 14, 15, 23 ⓘ Admission charge for performances and some exhibitions

Snafu ⓫ Comedy and live music from well-known performers are the keynotes of this amiable nightspot. ⓐ 1 Union Street ⓣ 01224 596111 ⓕ 01224 596116 ⓦ www.clubsnafu.com ⓔ info@clubsnafu.com ⓛ Normally 22.00–03.00 Wed–Mon, sometimes earlier; closed Tues ⓝ Bus: 1, 2, 13, 40, 50, 51, 251, 260, 263, 267, 268, 290, 291 ⓘ Admission charge

Soul Bar ⓬ Award-winning, trendy restaurant-café-bar which is open all day and which boasts what must be Aberdeen's most impressive cocktail list. ⓐ 333 Union Street ⓣ 01224 211150 ⓦ www.pbdevco.com ⓔ events@pbdevco.com ⓛ 09.00–24.00 Mon–Thur, 09.00–01.00 Sat, 10.00–24.00 Sun; food served daily 12.00–21.00 ⓝ Bus: 6, 11, 14, 15, 23

Old Aberdeen & Bridge of Don

Old Aberdeen lies little more than 1.5 km (1 mile) north of the city centre. It's dominated by the medieval buildings of **King's College**, which form the centre of the University of Aberdeen, and the spire of the venerable **St Machar's Cathedral**. The historic core of Old Aberdeen is a conservation area, with cobbled streets and a number of outstanding historic buildings. Just north of Old Aberdeen, **Seaton Park** is a wide urban green space on the south bank of the River Don. **King Street**, running north to south, connects Old Aberdeen with the city centre. It's an easy walk, but in case of bad weather, or late at night, there are frequent buses. At the northern end of King Street, a road bridge crosses the Don to the suburb of **Bridge of Don**, which is mainly residential but is also the home of the Aberdeen Science and Technology Park and Royal Aberdeen Golf Course. The 14th-century **Brig O' Balgownie**, crossing the Don from the north end of Don Street, north of Seaton Park, to Balgownie Road, is claimed to be the oldest bridge in Scotland.

Old Aberdeen is visibly student territory, but it's so close to the city centre that it doesn't have a lot of nightlife or shopping to call its own. Most residents head straight into the centre – not much more than 15 minutes' walk – for a night out or some retail therapy. The university campus has an acceptable on-site restaurant, but for a wider choice of places to eat or drink, head south into town or cross the river to Bridge of Don. For a breath of fresh air, the sands of **Aberdeen Beach** are less than a ten-minute walk away and for football lovers, **Pittodrie Stadium**, home of Aberdeen FC, is even closer.

SIGHTS & ATTRACTIONS

Cruickshank Botanic Garden

Founded in 1898 on 4 hectares (11 acres) of sheltered grounds, the Botanic Garden comprises a semi-wild arboretum of native and exotic trees and shrubs, rose gardens, azalea shrubberies, ponds, and lawns shaded by birch and beech trees. This lovely green space is at its best in summer and autumn, but it's a beautiful and tranquil place at any time of year. ⓐ The Canonry, St Machar Drive ⓣ 01224 274545 ⓦ www.abdn.ac.uk/botanic-garden ⓔ r.d.walker@abdn.ac.uk ⓛ 09.00–21.30 Mon–Fri & 14.00–21.30 Sat & Sun (May–Sept); 09.00–16.30 Mon–Fri, closed Sat & Sun (Oct–Apr) ⓝ Bus: 1, 2, 13, 14, 19, 20, 40

▲ *A centre of learning: King's College*

Glover House

This Victorian house was the home of Thomas Blake Glover, known to history as 'the Scottish Samurai'. Born in Fraserburgh in 1838, Glover moved to Aberdeen with his family aged six and was educated here. As an adventurous and ambitious young man, he travelled to Nagasaki in Japan at the age of 21, arriving just as that country began to open up to Western trade. Glover quickly built a fortune selling European arms and industrial equipment to Japan's nobles. He commissioned the Imperial Navy's first modern warships from an Aberdeen shipyard, imported the country's first steam locomotive, and founded the shipbuilding company that grew to become the industrial giant Mitsubishi. Glover died in 1911 in Japan, where

🔺 *The elegant Old Town House with the Mercat Cross*

he is still remembered as one of the key figures in the modernisation of Japan. In 2010, Glover House was closed for renovation. For details of reopening and guided-tour times, contact Aberdeenshire Council. ⓐ 79 Balgownie Road, Bridge of Don ⓘ 01224 664573 ⓦ www.aberdeencity.gov.uk ⓔ Jacqueline.rattray@aberdeenshire.gov.uk ⓝ Bus: 20 to end of line, then cross river by footbridge; or 1 or 2 to Balgownie Road ⓘ Admission charge

King's College

Only the most blasé of visitors can remain unimpressed by the complex of historic buildings that forms the quadrangle of King's College. The campus's iconic landmark is the Crown Tower, topped by a stone crown. Below it, the college's chapel boasts the best-preserved medieval interior of any Scottish church. The tombs of Bishop William Elphinstone, founder of King's College, and its first principal, the theologian and historian Hector Boyce, are beside the chancel. The campus includes the Cromwell Tower, the city's 17th-century observatory. The more modern New Building, dating from 1913, and Elphinstone Hall, built in 1930, dominate a second, newer quadrangle adjacent to the original campus and blend surprisingly well with their older neighbours. ⓐ High Street ⓘ 01224 272137 ⓦ www.abdn.ac.uk ⓛ 10.00–15.30 ⓝ Bus: 1, 2, 13, 20, 40, 50, 51, 251, 260, 263, 267, 268, 290, 291

Old Town House & the Mercat Cross

As an independent burgh until it merged with 'new' Aberdeen, Old Aberdeen had its own Town House. Built in 1789, this was where the town council met and was the centre of the burgh's mercantile life. It's an elegant Georgian edifice of pale grey granite, and is now part of the university. Outside, on the cobbled space that was Old Aberdeen's marketplace, stands the unassuming Mercat Cross, a stone pillar, which marked the very centre of the burgh. ⓐ High Street

St Machar's Cathedral

The history of Aberdeen's most important historic building goes back to the 6th century AD. Machar was a follower of Columba, the missionary saint who brought Christianity to Scotland; the little chapel he founded grew into one of the great religious sites of northern Scotland. Today, it is one of the finest surviving medieval fortified churches in Scotland, with a façade dominated by twin towers designed after the manner of 14th-century keeps. In the 16th century, these were capped by the spires that still grace them today. Two gloriously coloured windows – the St Machar Window and the Bishops' Window, both by the great Scottish stained-glass artist Douglas Strachan (1875–1950) – commemorate the cathedral's patron saint and the three medieval bishops who contributed most to its growth. ⓐ The Chanonry ⓣ 01224 485988 ⓦ www.stmachar.com ⓔ office@stmachar.com ⓛ 09.00–17.00 daily (Apr–Sept); 10.00–16.00 (Oct–Mar) ⓝ Bus: 20

Seaton Park

Just north of St Machar's Cathedral, Seaton Park is a wide green space bounded by an oxbow bend of the River Don. With formal flower beds, patches of woodland and a river-bank walk, it's a pleasant spot for a stroll or a picnic. At the northeast corner of the park stands a miniature castle, the Wallace Tower. The name is misleading – it has nothing to do with the legendary patriot William Wallace, but is a corruption of 'well-house'. It was the 'town lodging' of Sir Robert Keith of Benholm, brother of the Earl Marischal who founded Marischal College, and was built around

⬥ *The fortified, medieval St Machar's Cathedral*

1616 on the Nether Kirkgate, next to one of the city's wells. If it looks remarkably well preserved for its age, that's because it was carefully dismantled in 1964 to make way for a new Marks and Spencer's store and painstakingly rebuilt on its present site beside the Don. It isn't open to the public, but from the outside you can get a good impression of one of the typical 'Z-plan' fortified aristocratic homes of the early 17th century. ⓐ Don Street ⏰ 24 hrs daily Ⓝ Bus: 20

TAKING A BREAK

The Bobbin £ ⑱ This is the default student pub in Old Aberdeen, right across the street from the campus. If what you want is cheap beer, pub food, loud music and a variety of sports on TV, go for it. Anyone much over 25 may find it rather too

🔺 A cottage on the High Street of old Aberdeen

youthful, however. ⓐ 500 King Street ⓘ 01224 493318 ⓛ 11.00–
01.00 Mon–Sat, 12.30–23.00 Sun ⓝ Bus: 1, 2, 13, 20, 40, 50, 51, 251,
260, 263, 267, 268, 290, 291

Mains of Scotstown Inn £–££ ⓮ Appearances are deceptive.
Inside this sturdy old stone farm building is a classy modern
restaurant, complemented by an award-winning pub. The bar
serves classic pub grub, while the restaurant offers a more
comprehensive and sophisticated choice. ⓐ Jesmond Square,
Bridge of Don ⓘ 01224 825222 ⓦ www.restaurantsaberdeen.com
ⓛ Bar 11.00–23.00 Mon–Wed, 11.00–24.00 Thur–Sat, 12.30–23.00
Sun; restaurant 12.00–14.30 & 17.00–21.00 Mon–Fri, 12.00–21.00
Sat & Sun ⓝ Bus: 1, 2

The Parkway Inn £–££ ⓯ Spanking new place to eat just across
the river from Old Aberdeen. The Sunday carvery lunch is truly
excellent value, with a choice of at least two traditional roasts
with all the trimmings, but there's plenty more on offer during
the day and after dark. ⓐ Balgownie Road, Bridge of Don
ⓘ 01224 702460 ⓦ www.restaurantsaberdeen.com
ⓛ 12.00–14.30 & 17.00–21.00 Tues–Sat, 12.00–20.00 Sun, closed
Mon ⓝ Bus: 1, 2

Zeste £–££ ⓰ Aberdeen University's own on-campus bistro
offers breakfast, snacks and a lunch menu that includes good
salads, hearty soups, sandwiches, patés and dips, burgers, pasta
and vegetarian dishes. ⓐ Crombie Hall, King's College Campus
ⓘ 01224 273131 ⓦ www.abdn.ac.uk ⓛ 09.00–15.45, lunch 12.00–
14.00 ⓝ Bus: 1, 2, 13, 20, 40, 50, 51, 251, 260, 263, 267, 268, 290, 291

Aberdeen's seaside & the North Sea

The North Sea has shaped Aberdeen's history for more than a thousand years, and nowhere is the contrast between the city's past and present more apparent than in and around the harbour area. Here, ferries and cruise ships heading for the Northern Isles and Scandinavia share the quaysides with oil support vessels and the dwindling remnants of Aberdeen's fishing fleet. A headland stretching southwards protects

⬤ *Family fun at Codona's Amusement Park*

the main harbour from the full force of the sea. From here, **Aberdeen Beach** sweeps northwards for 3 km (2 miles) to the mouth of the River Don, with the city's Beach Esplanade running along its full length. Just inland are the windswept fairways of the King's Links golf course, while north of the Don are the challenging links of the world's sixth oldest golf course.

Looking south, Victoria Bridge crosses the Dee from the south end of Market Street to **Torry**, on the south bank. The foundations of the Torry Battery, a gun emplacement built in 1860, which was still in service during World War I and World War II, can still be seen at Torry Point, facing out to sea. South of the city, there are stretches of wild, windswept pebble beach and cliffs where seabirds roost and breed, and from the clifftops you might even be lucky enough to spot a passing school of dolphins or porpoises.

SIGHTS & ATTRACTIONS

Codona's Amusement Park

Operated by a family who opened Scotland's first funfair more than a century ago, Codona's Amusement Park offers all the outdoor fun of the fair with waltzers, rollercoaster rides, a big wheel, hot dogs and candy-floss. Indoors, Sunset Boulevard, Congo Golf and Pirate Island offer ten-pin bowling, dodgems, indoor golf, pool tables and a choice of bars. In short, good old-fashioned family fun – but with special 'student nights' on Mondays. ⓐ Beach Boulevard ❶ 01224 595910 ⓦ www.codonas.com ⓔ info@codonas.com ⓛ 10.00–24.00 Sun–Thur, 10.00–01.00 Fri & Sat Ⓝ Bus: 13A ❶ Admission charge

Dunnottar Castle

Dunnottar is around 16 km (10 miles) south of Aberdeen, but for those with half a day to spare this is a must-see historic attraction. Perched atop its grim crag jutting into the North Sea, ruined Dunnottar is one of the east coast's most striking castles. Seat of the Earls Marischal from the 14th century, its history is a bloody and dramatic tale of siege and massacre. Its breathtaking location has made it a favourite film and TV location – Mel Gibson played *Hamlet* here, directed by Franco Zeffirelli, in the 1990 version of Shakespeare's play. In April and May, multitudes of seabirds including puffins, guillemots and kittiwakes nest on the cliffs either side of the castle. ⓐ A92, 3 km (2 miles) south of Stonehaven ⓣ 01569 762173 ⓦ www.dunnottarcastle.co.uk ⓛ 09.00–18.00 daily (Apr–mid-Oct); 10.30–sunset Fri–Mon, closed Tues–Thur (Oct–Apr) ⓝ Bus: 107, 109, 117 to Stonehaven, then 113 to Dunnottar ⓘ Admission charge

Footdee

The contrast between Aberdeen's busy harbour and the 19th-century enclave of Footdee (pronounced 'Fittie') could not be greater. Just a short distance north of the industrial waterfront, with its ferry terminal, warehouses, fishing boats, and oil support vessels, Footdee is a picturesque and well-preserved piece of local history, with small, cosy cottages built around two small squares which occupy the headland north of the mouth of the harbour. Originally built for the families of fishing folk, these little stone houses are now much in demand with city-dwellers looking for a home with character close to the city centre. ⓐ North Square and South Square, Footdee ⓝ Bus: 13A

King's Links Golf Centre

Golf for the people! No membership is required to play this good old-fashioned east-coast links course, which is owned by the city. With plenty of time, you can play the par 71 eighteen-hole course. If you have less time, there's a par 21 six-hole course and also a multi-bay, floodlit driving range. ⓐ Golf Road ⓣ 01224 641577 ⓦ www.craig-group.com ⓔ info@kings-links.com ⓛ 09.00–21.30 Mon–Thur, 09.00–21.00 Fri, 09.00–17.30 Sat & Sun (Apr–Aug); 09.00–21.00 Mon–Fri, 09.00–17.30 Sat & Sun (Sept–Mar) ⓝ Bus: 1, 2, 13, 50, 51, 251, 260, 263, 267, 290, 291, 901 ⓘ Admission charge

Pittodrie Stadium

Pittodrie is a landmark for Scottish football. Built in 1899, it is the home of Aberdeen FC – also known as 'the Dons' and 'the Reds'. During their golden age in the early 1980s, the Reds became one of the top teams in European soccer, winning the European Cup Winners' Cup and the European Super Cup in 1983. Seating just over 22,000, it has the dubious distinction of being the chilliest ground in the UK. ⓐ Pittodrie St ⓣ 01224 631903 ⓦ www.afc.co.uk ⓔ feedback@afc.co.uk ⓛ contact club for fixtures ⓝ Bus: 1, 1A, 2, 2A, 15 ⓘ Admission charge

Royal Aberdeen Golf Club

Host to the Walker Cup in 2011, the Royal Aberdeen proudly claims to be the sixth-oldest golf club in the world, from its foundation in 1786. However, it took its present name only in 1815, and moved to its present home at Balgownie Links, overlooking the North Sea and the north bank of the Don, in

1888. The Royal Aberdeen claims to have invented the five-minute rule, limiting the time that can be spent hunting for a lost ball. Golfers accustomed to the manicured, architect-designed greens of *parvenu* golfing destinations such as Spain, the Algarve or Florida will find this classic Scottish links course a real challenge, with its dunes, grassy knolls, clumps of gorse and crosswinds ⓐ Balgownie Links, Links Road, Bridge of Don ① 01224 702751 ⓦ www.royalaberdeengolf.com ⓔ reservations@royalaberdeengolf.com ① 10.00–11.30 & 14.00–15.30 Mon, Wed, Fri, 11.04–12.00 & 14.00–15.30 Tues & Thur, 15.30–16.00 Sat & Sun (winter) & 15.30–18.00 Sat & Sun (summer) ⓝ Bus: 1, 2, 13, 50, 51, 251, 260, 263, 267, 290, 291, 901 ① Admission charge

● *The magnificently sited Dunnottar Castle, near Stonehaven*

CULTURE

Aberdeen Maritime Museum

This award-winning museum is housed in two historic buildings which are linked by a striking steel and glass building constructed in 1997. The museum houses a comprehensive collection that covers the history of seafaring, fishing and shipbuilding in Aberdeen and the northeast from medieval times through to the 21st century. Among the most striking exhibits is the 9-m (30-ft) high model of the Murchison North Sea oil platform. ⓐ Shiprow ⓣ 01224 337700 ⓦ www.aberdeencity.gov.uk ⓔ info@aagm.co.uk ⓛ 10.00–17.00 Tues–Sat, 12.00–15.00 Sun ⓝ Bus: 6, 11, 14, 15, 23

Cathedral Church of St Andrew

No less an expert than Sir John Betjeman praised the gracious architecture of the Cathedral Church, which was designed in 1816 by the prominent local architect Archibald Simpson. The talented Simpson was later commissioned by Prince Albert to design Balmoral Castle on Deeside for Queen Victoria, and his grand public buildings can be seen all over Scotland. ⓐ 28 King Street ⓣ 01224 640119 ⓦ www.cathedral.aberdeen.anglican.org ⓔ cathedral@aberdeen.anglican.org ⓛ 10.30–13.00 Sat, closed Sun–Fri (Jan–Dec); additionally 11.00–16.00 Tues–Fri (May–mid-Sept) ⓝ Bus: 6, 11, 14, 15, 23

Satrosphere Science Centre

Mainly aimed at parents with school-age children, Satrosphere pioneered hands-on science for kids in Scotland. Housed in the city's former tramsheds, it has more than 50 interactive exhibits and is a great place for a rainy day if you have children in tow. ⓐ The Tramsheds, 179 Constitution Street ⓣ 01224 640340 ⓦ www.satrosphere.net ⓔ info@satrosphere.net ⓛ 10.00–17.00 daily ⓝ Bus: 13A

RETAIL THERAPY

Aberdeen Maritime Museum Shop The Maritime Museum's shop is a great place to buy all sorts of nautical gifts and souvenirs, from model ships to fishermen's caps and T-shirts, prints, postcards and replica brass telescopes. ⓐ Shiprow ⓣ 01224 337700 ⓦ www.aberdeencity.gov.uk ⓔ info@aagm.co.uk ⓛ 10.00–17.00 Tues–Sat, 12.00–15.00 Sun ⓝ Bus: 6, 11, 14, 15, 23

King's Links Golf Centre Superstore The Golf Centre's huge 280-sq-m (3,000-sq-ft) sport superstore is staffed by experts and sells a vast assortment of clubs, footwear, accessories and clothing for men, women and junior golfers. ⓐ Golf Road ⓣ 01224 641577 ⓦ www.craig-group.com ⓔ info@kings-links.com ⓛ 09.00–21.30 Mon–Thur, 09.00–21.00 Fri, 09.00–17.30 Sat & Sun (Apr–Aug); 09.00–21.00 Mon–Fri, 09.00–17.30 Sat & Sun (Sept–Mar) ⓝ Bus: 1, 2, 13, 50, 51, 251, 260, 263, 267, 290, 291, 901

Satrosphere Science Shop The Satrosphere's shop sells educational toys, experiment kits, models, games and toys such as kites, gliders and hot-air balloons. Most of the goods on sale are aimed at children and young teenagers, but there are plenty

● *Enjoy some hands-on science at the Satrosphere Science Centre*

of fun objects for all. ⓐ 179 Constitution Street ① 01224 640340
ⓦ www.satrosphere.net ⓔ info@satrosphere.net ① 10.00–17.00
daily ⓝ Bus: 13A

TAKING A BREAK

The Fittie Bar £ ⑰ A harbour area institution for decades, this
old-fashioned pub is crammed with seafaring memorabilia. Its
clientele, too, seems to be mainly made up of seafaring men. It's
one of Aberdeen's last authentic pubs, and in the lounge bar
there are murals depicting the history of 'Fittie' (Footdee).
ⓐ 18 Wellington Street ① 01224 582911 ① 11.00–24.00 Mon–Sat,
12.30–23.00 Sun ⓝ Bus: 13A

Leading Lights Café £ The Aberdeen Maritime Museum's café serves soft drinks, a choice of teas and coffees, snacks, sandwiches, light meals and cakes. ⓐ Aberdeen Maritime Museum, Shiprow ⓣ 01224 337700 ⓦ www.aberdeencity.gov.uk ⓔ info@aagm.co.uk ⓛ 10.00–16.45 Tues–Sat, 12.00–14.45 Sun, closed Mon ⓝ Bus: 6, 11, 14, 15, 23

Sand Dollar Café £ ⓳ Light, bright modern diner with great sea views, serving breakfast (the 'full Scottish'), brunch, snacks such as panini, baked potatoes and sandwiches, and a bistro-style evening menu. ⓐ 2 Beach Esplanade ⓣ 01224 572288 ⓦ www.sanddollarcafe.com ⓔ garry@sanddollarcafe.com ⓛ Café 09.00–18.00 Sun–Wed, 09.00–16.00 Thur–Sat; Bistro 18.00–01.00 Thur–Sat (last orders for meals 21.00, drinks for diners until 01.00) ⓝ Bus: 14

Tramsheds Coffee Shop £ ⓴ Serving the ubiquitous Starbucks coffee-and-cakes formula, this coffee shop is a good place to take a break after visiting the Science Centre. ⓐ Satrosphere Science Centre, 179 Constitution Street ⓣ 01224 640340 ⓦ www.satrosphere.net ⓔ info@satrosphere.net ⓛ 10.00–17.00 daily ⓝ Bus: 13A

Frankie & Benny's £–££ ㉑ Part of a chain that tries to summon up the spirit of New York's 'Little Italy' in its heyday with 1950s music, diner-style booths and a classic Italo-American menu featuring pizzas, pasta, grilled ribs and burgers. ⓐ Queen's Links Leisure Park, Beach Esplanade ⓣ 01224 590394 ⓦ www.frankieandbennys.com ⓛ 11.00–23.00 Mon–Sat, 11.00–22.30 Sun ⓝ Bus: 13A

Silver Darling £££ ❷ Fabulously fresh seafood, lovingly prepared, is the keynote of the Silver Darling, which is considered by many people to be Aberdeen's finest independent restaurant. ❸ North Pier, Pocra Quay ❶ 01224 576229 ⓦ www.silverdarling.co.uk ❹ 12.00–13.30 Mon–Fri & 18.30–21.30 Mon–Sat, closed Sun ❷ Bus: 13A

🔻 *A beautiful day on Aberdeen's beach*

AFTER DARK

Aberdeen Exhibition and Conference Centre ㉓ Most of Aberdeen's regular nightlife is to be found downtown, but it's the AECC's Press and Journal Arena that plays host to visiting rock gods, dinosaurs and goddesses ranging from David Bowie, Neil Young, Status Quo and Paul Weller to the Arctic Monkeys, the Kaiser Chiefs and Lady Gaga. ⓐ Exhibition Avenue, Bridge of Don ① 01224 824824 ⓦ aecc.co.uk ⓔ aecc@aecc.co.uk ⓛ Varies for performances and events ① Admission charge

Beach Ballroom ㉔ Aberdeen's grand old municipal ballroom is now used mainly for performances by kitsch tribute bands playing favourites from stars including The Beatles, Tom Jones and Neil Diamond. ⓐ The Esplanade ① 01224 647647 ⓦ www.beachballroom.com ⓛ See website for programme ⓝ Bus: 14 ① Admission charge

Motown Soul Bar ㉕ This club-style bar overlooking the waterfront from its top-floor location on the Esplanade hosts a range of soul and salsa nights in association with the city centre flagship club Snafu (see page 59). ⓐ The Esplanade ① 01224 583388 ⓛ 11.00–23.00 Sun–Thur, 11.00–24.00 Fri & Sat ⓝ Bus: 14

● *Balmoral Castle is the royal family's favourite summer residence*

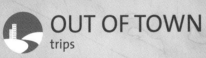
OUT OF TOWN
trips

Royal Deeside & the Cairngorms

The River Dee, which flows into the North Sea at Aberdeen, rises in the Cairngorm Mountains and flows through a lushly wooded valley that is dotted with charming small towns and villages. It's not surprising that it was love at first sight for Queen Victoria when she and her consort Prince Albert first visited Deeside in 1848. Since then, her successors have visited every summer, and vast numbers of visitors follow in their footsteps each year. In July and August, spots like Braemar and Ballater are thronged with visitors, but outside high season this is a beautiful part of the world – and even in the busiest months, energetic visitors can escape the crowds by heading for the hills and moors of the Cairngorms.

GETTING THERE

With a rented car, Braemar is about 100 km (65 miles) or 90 minutes' drive from Aberdeen. It is also possible to visit Braemar, Ballater, Crathie and other points en route by coach (see page 91), and there are numerous escorted coach tours from Aberdeen all year round.

SIGHTS & ATTRACTIONS

Ballater

This charming little market town is a popular stop on the way to Balmoral Castle, holiday home of the British royal family. Replete with souvenir shops and cafés, it is a hotbed of 'tartan tourism' but it's still a good place to stop for refreshments. Its main attraction is the Old Royal Station, where a full-scale replica of the royal railway carriage used by Queen Victoria on her visits stands outside a restored 19th-century railway station. Inside, the opulent royal waiting room (built specially for Her Majesty) houses an exhibition of Victorian photos and railway memorabilia. ⓐ Old Royal Station, Station Square, Ballater ⓣ 01339 755306 ⓛ 09.00–18.00 daily (June & Sept); 09.30–19.00 daily (July & Aug); 10.00–18.00 daily (Oct–May) ⓘ Admission charge

Balmoral Castle

Prince Albert, Queen Victoria's consort, bought this Highland estate as a present for the queen. Albert commissioned an Aberdeen architect to build the fairytale mansion that is still the royal family's favourite summer getaway. Highland landscapes and portraits of royal ancestors adorn the ballroom, which is open to the public when the royals are not in residence, along with the gardens and exhibitions. ⓐ Crathie, 13 km (8 miles) west of Ballater ⓣ 01339 742354 ⓦ www.balmoralcastle.com ⓛ 10.00–17.00 daily (Mar–July); closed Aug–Oct, winter tours by appointment (see website for details) ⓘ Admission charge

Braemar

Braemar comes into its own during the annual Royal Braemar Gathering, traditionally held on the first Saturday in September with a number of the royal family in attendance. This is the biggest and grandest of all Scotland's Highland gatherings, with kilted pipers, dancers, and caber-tossers showing off their skills and strength. Braemar Castle, a miniature fortress that housed

an army garrison until 1831, has been restored by local volunteers. **Royal Braemar Gathering** ⓐ Braemar ⓣ 01339 741098 ⓦ braemargathering.org ⓛ 1st Saturday in September ⓘ Admission charge. **Braemar Castle** ⓐ Braemar ⓣ 01339 741219 ⓦ www.braemarcastle.co.uk ⓛ 11.00–16.00 Sat & Sun, closed Mon–Fri (May, June; Sept & Oct); 11.00–16.00 Wed, Sat & Sun, closed Mon, Tues, Thur, Fri (July & Aug) ⓘ Admission charge

Cairngorms National Park

Braemar, Ballater and Balmoral all lie within the boundaries of the Cairngorms National Park, Britain's greatest wilderness area. An area of spectacular natural beauty, it contains the largest expanse of arctic mountain landscape in the UK and provides a refuge for red deer, golden eagles, pine martens, ospreys and ptarmigans. It's easily accessible, and for fit walkers the summit of Lochnagar (1,154 m/3,787 ft above sea level) is a tough but feasible

● *The Cairngorms in winter, viewed from Loch Morlich*

summer's-day walk from Crathie or Braemar. ❹ Access from the A93 from Aberdeen ❶ 01479 870521 ❺ 24 hours daily

CULTURE

Braemar Highland Heritage Centre

The Heritage Centre's audiovisual show highlights Braemar's history and its royal connections and displays of Highland dress celebrate all things tartan and traditional. ❹ Mar Road ❶ 01339 741944 ❺ 01339 741944 ❻ bhhc@lochcarron.com ❺ 09.00–17.00 daily (Apr–Oct); 10.00–16.00 daily (Nov–Mar)

RETAIL THERAPY

Ballater and Braemar are replete with shops selling souvenirs, tartan clothing, knitwear, 'antiques' and memorabilia of all kinds.

TAKING A BREAK

The Green Inn ££ ㉖ Award-winning restaurant with rooms, which prides itself on offering the best of local meat, vegetables, fruit and seafood. ❹ 9 Victoria Road, Ballater ❶ 01339 755701 ❼ www.green-inn.com ❺ 19.00–21.00 daily, booking essential

The Spirit Restaurant ££ ㉗ The restaurant of the Auld Kirk (a former church converted into a small, intimate and charming boutique hotel) is the best place on Deeside for elegant evening dining. ❹ 31 Braemar Road, Ballater ❶ 01339 755762 ❺ 18.30–22.30 Mon–Sat, closed Sun

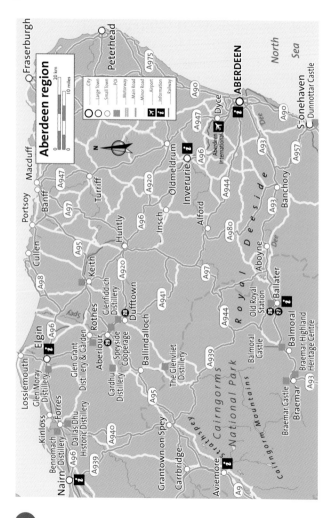

Aberdeen region

0 — 20 km
0 — 10 miles

| City |
| Large Town |
| Small Town |
| POI |
| Motorway |
| Main Road |
| Minor Road |
| Airport |
| Information |
| Railway |

Fraserburgh

Peterhead

A975

North Sea

Macduff

Portsoy

Banff

A947

A97

Turriff

A920

Oldmeldrum

A96

Insch

Inverurie

A947

Aberdeen International

Dyce

ABERDEEN

A90

A90

Stonehaven

Dunnottar Castle

A957

A92

A90

Banchory

Dee

Deeside

Aboyne

Alford

A980

A944

A93

Cullen

A98

A95

Keith

Glenfiddich Distillery

A941

Dufftown

A920

Huntly

Rothes

Aberlour

Speyside Cooperage

Ballindalloch

The Glenlivet Distillery

A939

A97

Royal

Old Royal Station

Ballater

Balmoral Castle

Balmoral

Braemar Highland Heritage Centre

A93

Braemar Castle

Braemar

Elgin

Lossiemouth

Glen Moray Distillery

Forres

Glen Grant Distillery & Garden

Cardhu Distillery

A95

Grantown on Spey

Strathspey

Cairngorms National Park

Balmoral Mountains

Kinloss

Dallas Dhu Historic Distillery

Benromach Distillery

Nairn

A939

A940

Carrbridge

A9

Aviemore

A96

N

The Speyside Malt Whisky Trail

The lovely valley of Strathspey is the heart of the malt whisky industry, and the streams that flow into the River Spey provide the pure, clear water that is essential to the making of some of the world's finest malts. There are more than 40 distilleries dotted around Speyside, and many of them (including all those listed here) are part of the world's only Malt Whisky Trail (Ⓦ www.maltwhiskytrail.com), offering tours, tastings and the opportunity to buy the product. Even for those who aren't whisky fanciers, Speyside's pretty countryside makes for a pleasant outing.

GETTING THERE

Speyside is around 100 km (65 miles) from Aberdeen on the A96 main road, a drive that takes about 90 minutes. Allow around six hours to explore the region, visiting several of the distilleries and pausing for lunch. Alternatively, join a tailor-made minibus tour of the Malt Whisky Trail, which allows everyone in your party to sample the product. **Castle Tours** ❶ 07525 865348 Ⓦ www.castle-tours.co.uk and **Duncan's Flexible Tours** ❶ 0800 44 88 369 Ⓦ www.duncans-flexitours.co.uk

SIGHTS & ATTRACTIONS

Benromach Distillery
Benromach is the smallest working distillery on Speyside and offers tours, tastings and a gift shop. ❸ Invererne Road, Forres ❶ 01309 675968 🕐 09.30–17.00 Mon–Sat, closed Sun (May &

Sept); 09.30–17.00 Mon–Sat, 12.00–16.00 Sun (June–Aug); 10.00–16.00 Mon–Fri, closed Sat & Sun (Oct–Apr, except Christmas and Jan) ⓦ www.benromach.com ❶ Admission charge

Cardhu Distillery

Cardhu's visitor centre reveals the remarkable story of the only malt whisky distillery to have been founded by a woman. As well as producing its own single malt whisky, Cardhu also supplies malt whisky that is used to create the world-famous Johnnie Walker blended whiskies. ⓐ Knockando, Aberlour ❶ 01479 874635 ⓦ www.discovering-distilleries.com ⓛ 10.00–17.00 Mon–Fri, closed Sat & Sun (Apr–June); 10.00–17.00 Mon–Sat, 12.00–16.00 Sun (July–Sept); 11.00–15.00 Mon–Fri, closed Sat & Sun (Oct–Mar) ❶ Admission charge

Dallas Dhu Historic Distillery

Dallas Dhu no longer makes whisky, but is maintained by Historic Scotland as a well-preserved example of an old-style working distillery. It opened in 1898, and a free dram is still offered to visitors. ⓐ Mannachie Road, Forres ❶ 01309 676548 ⓦ www.historic-scotland.gov.uk ⓛ 09.30–17.30 daily (Apr–Sept); 09.30–16.30 daily (Oct); 09.30–16.30 Sat–Tues, closed Wed–Fri (Nov–Mar) ❶ Admission charge

Glenfiddich Distillery

Glenfiddich is one of the most famous and best-loved of Speyside malts and is exported all over the world. Its modern distillery is a state-of-the-art visitor attraction, with guided tours, a sophisticated visitor centre and a whisky bar and coffee

THE SPEYSIDE MALT WHISKY TRAIL

shop. There's also a connoisseur's tasting tour, for which advance booking is recommended. ⓐ Dufftown ⓣ 01340 820373 ⓦ www.glenfiddich.com ⓛ 09.30–16.30 Mon–Sat, 12.00–16.30 Sun ⓘ Admission charge for Connoisseur's Tour

Glen Grant Distillery & Garden

This venerable distillery, which was founded in 1840, is one of Speyside's most charming visitor attractions, and is surrounded by beautifully laid out Victorian gardens. ⓐ Elgin Road, Rothes ⓣ 01340 83211 ⓦ www.glengrant.com ⓛ 09.30–17.00 Mon–Sat, 12.00–17.00 Sun (Feb–Dec) ⓘ Admission charge; children under 8 not admitted to production areas

The Glenlivet Distillery

The Glenlivet is another of Speyside's best-known malt whiskies. It was the first licensed whisky distiller in the Scottish Highlands. Guided tours end with a complimentary glass, and there is also a gift shop and coffee shop. ⓐ Glenlivet, Ballindalloch ⓣ 01340 821720 ⓦ www.maltwhiskydistilleries.com ⓣ 09.30–16.00 Mon–Sat, Sun 12.00–16.00 (Apr–Oct) ⓘ Admission charge

Glen Moray Distillery

Glen Moray has a much lower profile than some of its bigger neighbours along the banks of the Spey, but its classic single malt is highly regarded by those in the know. ⓐ Bruceland Road, Elgin ⓣ 01343 550900 ⓦ www.glenmoray.com ⓛ 09.00–17.00 Mon–Fri, closed Sat & Sun (Oct–Apr); 09.00–17.00 Mon–Fri, 10.00–16.30 Sat, closed Sun (May–Sept) ⓘ Admission charge

RETAIL THERAPY

Gordon & Macphail All the distilleries sell their own malts and blends, but this Elgin shop has perhaps the largest choice of whiskies in Scotland, as well as fine wines and liqueurs.
ⓐ 58–60 South Street, Elgin ☏ 01343 545110
Ⓦ www.gordonandmacphail.com ⏱ 09.00–17.00 Mon–Sat, closed Sun

Johnstons Cashmere Visitor Centre Soft and cosy cashmere scarves, sweaters, gloves and headgear to buy, as well as guided tours of the mill. ⓐ Newmill, Elgin ☏ 01343 554099
Ⓦ www.johnstonscashmere.com ⏱ 09.00–17.30 Mon–Sat, 11.00–17.00 Sun

TAKING A BREAK

La Faisanderie ££ ㉘ The smartest and best place for dinner on the Whisky Trail, serving fine local produce with a French accent.
ⓐ Balvenie Street, The Square, Dufftown ☏ 01340 821273
⏱ 18.00–20.30 Mon, Wed & Thur, 12.00–13.30 & 19.00–21.00 Fri & Sat, 12.00–13.30 & 18.00–20.30 Sun, closed Tues

The Mash Tun ££ ㉙ This gastropub serves good solid grub and has (surprise, surprise) an extensive choice of whiskies.
ⓐ 8 Broomfield Square, Aberlour ☏ 01340 881771 ⏱ 11.30–23.00 Mon–Sat, 12.00–23.00 Sun

---

▶ *Mercat Cross: information signs explain local sights and history*

PRACTICAL
information

PRACTICAL INFORMATION

Directory

GETTING THERE

By air

You can fly to Aberdeen from London and several regional British airports. The flight time is around 90 minutes from London (compared with 7–8 hours by rail and more than 12 hours by coach). Airlines serving Aberdeen include **British Airways** ( www.ba.com); **bmi** ( www.flybmi.com); **Eastern Airways** ( www.easternairways.com); **easyJet** ( www.easyjet.com); and **FlyBe** ( www.flybe.com). For a comprehensive list of airlines and routes to Aberdeen, see the Aberdeen Airport website.

Aberdeen Airport Dyce, Aberdeen 0870 040 0006 www.aberdeenairport.com

Many people are aware that air travel emits CO_2, which contributes to climate change. You may be interested in the possibility of lessening the environmental impact of your flight through the charity **Climate Care** (www.jpmorganclimatecare.com), which offsets your CO_2 by funding environmental projects around the world.

By rail

The east coast rail journey from London King's Cross to Aberdeen (via Leeds, York, Newcastle, Edinburgh and Dundee) takes 7–8 hours. There are at least three direct trains daily, as well as more frequent services with connections via Edinburgh. Overnight sleeper services are also available.

East Coast 08457 48950 www.eastcoast.co.uk
First ScotRail 08457 48950 www.scotrail.co.uk

By coach

There are coach services to Aberdeen from all over the UK. The journey time from London is around 12 hours.

CityLink ❶ 0871 266 3333 Ⓦ www.citylink.co.uk
Megabus ❶ 0900 160 1900 Ⓦ www.megabus.com
National Express ❶ 08717 818178 Ⓦ www.nationalexpress.com

HEALTH, SAFETY & CRIME

Visitors to Aberdeen are unlikely to encounter any major health or security issues. Violent crime, usually alcohol-related, does occur in the city centre's most popular nightlife areas, especially late at night at weekends. The usual rules apply: avoid confrontation with anyone who appears to be looking for a fight.

Emergencies

Ambulance, Fire, Police: ❶ 999
Accident and Emergency: Aberdeen Royal Hospitals ⓐ Foresterhill ⏱ 01224 681818
NHS 24 Medical Advice ❶ 08454 242424
Grampian Police (including Lost Property) ⓐ Queen Street ❶ 0845 600 5700

OPENING HOURS

Shops: 09.00–17.30 Mon–Sat. Some shops and department stores also open later until 19.00 or 20.00 on Thursdays. Many smaller newsagents and general stores open on Sunday morning from 08.30–12.30. Most larger malls and shopping centres open on Sunday from 12.00–18.00. Large supermarkets open on Sunday 09.30–18.00, but alcohol is not sold in stores before 12.30 on Sundays.

Banks: most banks open 09.30–16.30 Mon–Fri. Some city-centre branches also open 10.30–16.30 Sat.

Offices: most offices open 09.00–17.00 Mon–Fri.

Attractions: most attractions are open 10.00–17.00 with shorter opening hours on Sun.

TOILETS

There are adequate toilet facilities in the railway and bus stations and at several city-centre locations. These normally cost 20p (pay at turnstile). Free, clean toilets can be found in museums, department stores and shopping centres. Cafés that do not serve alcoholic drinks are not required to provide toilets (though some do); toilet facilities in pubs are for the use of patrons only.

CHILDREN

Children are welcome in virtually all eating places (except perhaps for a few of the top-class hotel restaurants) and in some pubs. Many eateries offer children's menus. There are plenty of visitor attractions geared specifically for children, including swimming pools with water slides (see page 21) and Codona's Sunset Boulevard Amusement Park (see page 69), while the long, sandy beach is a great place for children of all ages in summer.

TRAVELLERS WITH DISABILITIES

Aberdeen caters quite well for wheelchair users, with wheelchair ramps at bus and coach stations and on most streets, elevator access to shopping centres, and wheelchair-accessible taxis. Aberdeen City Council provides a Dial-a-Bus service on demand for wheelchair users. For details of locally available assistance for wheelchair users and other visitors with disabilities, contact **Horizons Grampian** ⓐ 2 Eday Walk ⓣ 01224 556873 ⓦ www.horizonsgrampian.co.uk

FURTHER INFORMATION

The Aberdeen Visitor Information Centre is centrally located on Union Street, close to the bus and railway stations, and provides an accommodation booking service and a range of leaflets, guidebooks and maps. The helpful staff also offer advice on where to go, what to do and places to eat. The same office also offers a similar range of services and information on the northeast and all of Scotland.

Aberdeen Visitor Information Centre ⓐ 23 Union Street ⓣ 01224 288828 ⓦ www.aberdeen-grampian.com ⓛ 09.30–17.00 Mon–Sat, closed Sun (Sept–June); 09.00–18.00 Mon–Sat, 10.00–16.00 Sun (July & Aug)

BACKGROUND READING

A Scots Quair by Lewis Grassic Gibbon (Canongate Classics, 1995) A moving trilogy that eulogises the vanishing rural culture of northeast Scotland in the early 20th century. The third book, *Grey Granite*, first published in 1934, is set in Aberdeen.

Cold Granite, *Dying Light* and *Broken Skin* by Stuart MacBride (HarperCollins, 2005, 2007, 2009) Three gritty crime novels set in and around Aberdeen.

ACKNOWLEDGEMENTS

The photographs in this book were taken by Cezare White for Thomas Cook Publishing, to whom the copyright belongs, except for the following: Aberdeen City Council page 46; Aberdeen Music Hall page 19; Balmoral Castle page 79; iStockphoto.com pages 5 (fintastique), 26–7 (Elnur), 28 (Gannet77), 38–9 (abzee), 37, 44, 49 & 53 (onfilm); Shutterstock pages 50 (Matt Gore), 61 (Creative Hearts), 65 & 72 (Bill McKelvie), 77 (Othman Photography), 82 (Gail Johnson).

Project editor: Rosalind Munro
Copy editor: Cath Senker
Layout: Paul Queripel
Proofreaders: Ceinwen Sinclair & Penny Isaac
Indexer: Zoë Ross

AUTHOR BIOGRAPHY

Zoë Ross is an editor and travel journalist, and author of a number of guidebooks including Thomas Cook city guides to Edinburgh and Glasgow. London-born, she now lives in Edinburgh.

Send your thoughts to
books@thomascook.com

- Found a great bar, club, shop or must-see sight that we don't feature?
- Like to tip us off about any information that needs a little updating?
- Want to tell us what you love about this handy little guidebook and more importantly how we can make it even handier?

Then here's your chance to tell all! Send us ideas, discoveries and recommendations today and then look out for your valuable input in the next edition of this title.

Email the above address (stating the title) or write to:
pocket guides Series Editor, Thomas Cook Publishing, PO Box 227, Coningsby Road, Peterborough PE3 8SB, UK.